GIANT DINOSAURS

THE BIGGEST REPTILES TO EVER WALK THE EARTH!

PAUL HARRISON

WHAT IS A DINOSAUR?

The word "dinosaur" means "terrible lizard," although a dinosaur is not a lizard but a type of reptile. There were hundreds of different types of dinosaur and they were real record breakers—the biggest, heaviest, longest, tallest creatures ever to have walked the planet. The first dinosaur remains were found in Connecticut in the early 19th century, followed by more discoveries in southern England. Since then, dinosaur fossils have been discovered all over the world.

Quaesitosaurus

Remember, not all dinosaurs were alive at the same time. Different species appeared and disappeared during the dinosaur era. For example, *Brachiosaurus* (see page 14) was not around at the same time as *Alamosaurus* or *Hadrosaurus* (see pages 8 and 16).

Dinosaurs are a large yet very specific group of creatures. To qualify, an animal has to satisfy a number of criteria:

1. It must have lived during the Mesozoic era, which is divided into three periods, called the Triassic, Jurassic, and Cretaceous. The Triassic lasted from 245 million years ago (mya) to 208 mya, the Jurassic from 208 mya to 145 mya, and the Cretaceous from 145 mya to the end of the dinosaurs (65 mya).

2. It must be a reptile, although not all reptiles are dinosaurs. For example, lizards are reptiles, but they are not dinosaurs.

3. Its legs must be located below its body, giving it an erect stance, as opposed to sticking out from the sides, like those of a crocodile.

4. It must have lived on land, not in the air like pterosaurs, or in the water like swimming reptiles.

Hadrosaurus

GIGANOTOSAURUS

When *Giganotosaurus* was first discovered in Argentina, it started a big debate—was this dinosaur the biggest meat-eater ever?

Biggest of all

Many paleontologists believe that *Giganotosaurus* was the largest of all the dinosaur carnivores—even larger than *Tyrannosaurus rex*. From findings made so far, it certainly seems to have been longer and taller than its more famous rival. However, it also seems to have been more lightly built than *Tyrannosaurus rex*, so the argument continues about who was the king of the meat-eaters.

TRIASSIC | JURASSIC | CRETACEOUS

The *Giganotosaurus* discovered in Argentina in 1993 had a larger skull and thigh bone than the biggest *T. rex*!

Big appetite

It is no surprise to learn that these giant carnivores had an appetite to match their size. Discoveries of the remains of other large dinosaur species in *Giganotosaurus* territory suggest that even huge herbivores were a potential meal for this giant.

Fact File

How to say it JI-gah-no-tuh-SORE-us
Meaning of name Giant southern lizard
Family Allosauridae
Period Mid-Cretaceous
Where found Argentina
Height 10 feet (3 meters)
Length 43 feet (13 meters)
Weight 6 tons (5,400 kilograms)
Food Meat
Special features Biggest carnivore of all?

ALAMOSAURUS

With its long neck and whippy tail, *Alamosaurus* looked much like any other sauropod. However, it was rare because it was the only type of sauropod to be found in North America at this time.

A long way from home?

Sauropods were the giants of the dinosaur age. The biggest animals to have walked on land, they were a type of dinosaur with long necks and tails, but small heads. Their numbers peaked during the Jurassic period, but by the late Cretaceous, they had disappeared from North America, apart from *Alamosaurus*, which was found in Texas, Utah, and New Mexico. Some experts believe that *Alamosaurus* wandered up from South America, where more sauropods could still have been found at the time.

Bulky body

The largest sauropods, like *Brachiosaurus*, were about 53 feet (16 meters) high and weighed over 88 tons (80,000 kilograms). Although *Alamosaurus* was much smaller, it was still big enough! Remarkably, it could even stand on its hind legs to feed on tasty leaves that might otherwise have been out of reach.

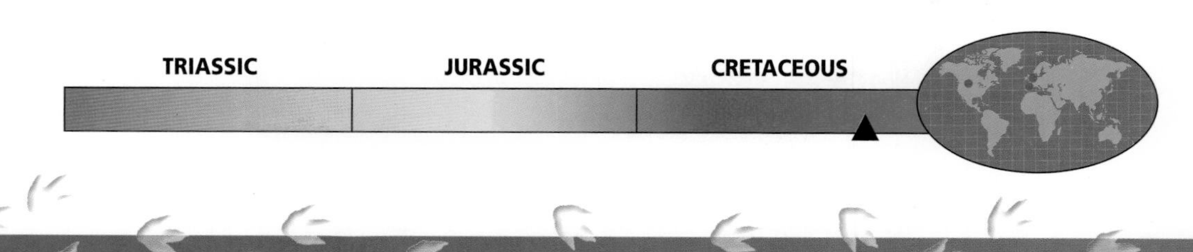

Despite its size, the powerful back legs of *Alamosaurus* could take its full weight when stretching to reach the topmost branches of trees.

SPINOSAURUS

This dinosaur might look a bit odd, but you wouldn't have wanted to say that to its face—this late Cretaceous predator was even longer than *Giganotosaurus*.

Sail

The most striking feature of *Spinosaurus* was the huge sail on its back. This wasn't for any kind of defensive purpose—a meat-eater like this had little to fear—instead, it was used to regulate the dinosaur's temperature. Blood was pumped around the sail, where it was either heated in the sun or cooled in the shade; this, in turn, controlled the temperature of *Spinosaurus*. Although sails were a relatively rare feature, they were found on other dinosaurs, as well as on reptiles such as *Dimetrodon*, which were around even earlier than the dinosaurs.

TRIASSIC JURASSIC CRETACEOUS

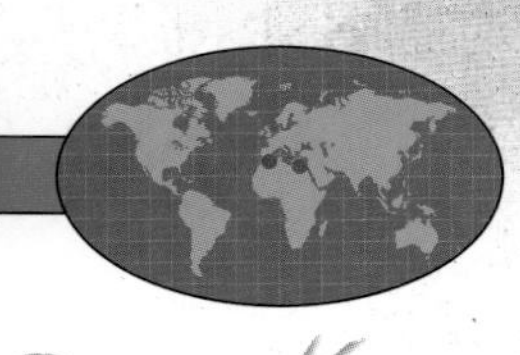

Fact File

How to say it SPINE-oh-SORE-us
Meaning of name Thorn lizard
Family Spinosauridae
Period Late Cretaceous
Where found Egypt, Morocco
Height 16 feet 6 inches (5 meters)
Length 53 feet (16 meters)
Weight 4 tons (3,600 kilograms)
Food Meat
Special features Large sail

Something fishy

Spinosaurus was a fish-eating dinosaur that was found near water. As there were few dinosaurs with a taste for fish, *Spinosaurus* had little competition at mealtimes and a big supply always to hand.

Although *Spinosaurus* loved fish, when it fancied a change it would snap up anything else that came within reach.

BARYONYX

With a mouth packed full of sharp teeth and with claws over 1 foot (0.3 meters) long, this large dinosaur looks like one mean customer. However, *Baryonyx* spent most of its time fishing, rather than terrifying the daylights out of other Cretaceous dinosaurs.

Gone fishin'

Like *Spinosaurus, Baryonyx* is the one of the few fish-eating dinosaurs that we know of. It was perfectly designed for this diet, with its long, crocodile-like snout—an ideal fish-catching tool. Or it would help itself to lunch by scooping fish out of the water, bear-style, with a swipe of its mighty claws.

They were believed to have eaten only fish, until the remains of a young *Iguanodon* were found in the stomach of a dead *Baryonyx*.

Fact File

How to say it baa-ree-ON-iks
Meaning of name Heavy claw
Family Spinosauridae
Period Early Cretaceous
Where found England, Spain
Height 8 feet (2.5 meters)
Length 33 feet (10 meters)
Weight 2 tons (1,800 kilograms)
Food Meat and fish
Special features Long snout and claws

A first for England

The remains of *Baryonyx* were first discovered in England and were a doubly important discovery: not only was it a new type of dinosaur, it was also the first fish-eating dinosaur to be found there.

BRACHIOSAURUS

One of the biggest, most famous dinosaurs of all time, *Brachiosaurus* was a true giant of the Jurassic world.

Going up

Besides its long neck, another contributing factor to the extreme height of *Brachiosaurus* was the fact that its front legs were considerably longer than its back ones. This gave *Brachiosaurus* an unusual upright stance and a marked advantage. As any giraffe knows, the youngest, juiciest shoots are at the top of a tree, and, if you're the tallest, you're the one who gets to eat them.

Fact File

How to say it BRAK-ee-oh-SORE-us
Meaning of name Arm lizard
Family Brachiosauridae
Period Late Jurassic
Where found Algeria, Portugal, Tanzania, USA
Height 53 feet (16 meters)
Length 99 feet (30 meters)
Weight 88 tons (80,000 kilograms)
Food Plants
Special features Extreme height

A Brachiosaurus's leg was around five times longer than that of an ostrich, the biggest bird around today.

TRIASSIC | JURASSIC | CRETACEOUS

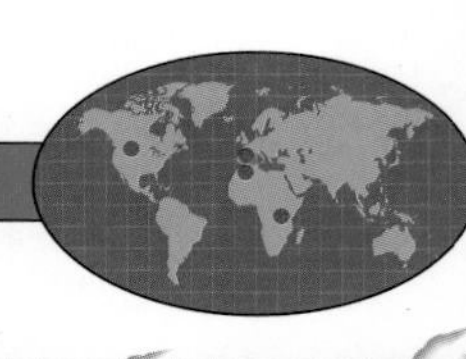

Pumping iron

Paleontologists are puzzled by how *Brachiosaurus* managed to walk around without fainting: with a head so far away from its body, getting blood to the brain must have been really difficult. Did it perhaps have two hearts? Probably not, but this dinosaur must have had an extremely powerful heart to get the blood all the way up to its brain. Unfortunately, we just don't know for sure.

HADROSAURUS

One of the first dinosaurs to be discovered in the USA, studies of *Hadrosaurus* have provided much of what we know about dinosaurs today.

Strength in numbers

Like many plant-eaters, *Hadrosaurus* lived in herds. Group living was a simple defense against attack from predators—it was much easier to spot any danger lurking close by if many animals were on the lookout rather than just one.

Swimmer

For a long time, paleontologists wondered whether dinosaurs such as *Hadrosaurus* spent most of their time in water. They had paddle-like hands and tails, well suited to propelling them through the water. Their remains are often found beside rivers. We now know that *Hadrosaurus* spent its time feeding near riverbanks but actually lived on land. However, *Hadrosaurus* was capable of swimming, so it could escape by water if a predator came too near.

Fact File

How to say it HA-drow-SORE-us
Meaning of name Heavy lizard
Family Hadrosauridae
Period Late Cretaceous
Where found USA
Height 10 feet (3 meters)
Length 26 feet (8 meters)
Weight 2.2 tons (2,000 kilograms)
Food Plants
Special features Paddle-like hands and tail

TRIASSIC | JURASSIC | CRETACEOUS

With rows of up to a thousand small teeth lined up to chomp through tough plants, *Hadrosaurus* had more teeth than any other dinosaur.

DIPLODOCUS

One of the most famous dinosaurs of all was *Diplodocus*, a huge but gentle and relatively slender giant. It traveled in herds, constantly on the move to find new grazing areas.

Long neck and tail

The most obvious feature of *Diplodocus* was its extremely long neck and tail. Its neck was about 26 feet (8 meters) long, but its tiny head measured less than 3 feet 3 inches (1 meter). The tail was as impressive as the neck and made an effective whiplike weapon for repelling predators.

Paleontologists believe that *Diplodocus* was partial to ferns in its diet.

Fact File

How to say it di-PLO-do-KUS
Meaning of name Double beam
Family Diplodocidae
Period Late Jurassic
Where found USA
Height 16 feet (5 meters)
Length 89 feet (27 meters)
Weight 12 tons (11,000 kilograms)
Food Plants
Special features Long neck and tail

TRIASSIC JURASSIC CRETACEOUS

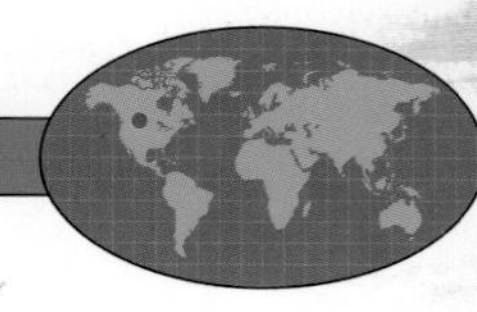

Ground feeder

Not all long-necked dinosaurs ate leaves from the treetops, and *Diplodocus* was a good example of this. Its front legs were shorter than its hind legs, so its neck naturally pointed down rather than up. The extreme length of its neck allowed *Diplodocus* to graze over a large area of ground without having to move its position.

IGUANODON

This plant-eating herd dweller was the second dinosaur ever to be named. It lived across a large part of the Northern Hemisphere.

Thumb spike

One of *Iguanodon*'s unusual features was its thumb spike—a horny digit on each hand where you might have expected the thumb to be. Paleontologists are still divided over the function of this spike. Some claim it was for defense and would have been used to stab an attacking predator. Others are less sure of its effectiveness as a weapon. Perhaps it was for digging up plants or pulling down branches?

Fact File

How to say it ig-WHA-no-don
Meaning of name Iguana tooth
Family Iguanodontidae
Period Early Cretaceous
Where found Belgium, England, Germany, Spain, USA
Height 16 feet 5 inches (5 meters)
Length 33 feet (10 meters)
Weight 4.4 tons (4,000 kilograms)
Food Plants
Special features Thumb spikes

The plant-eating *Iguanodon* had tough teeth in its beak-like mouth for grinding up plants.

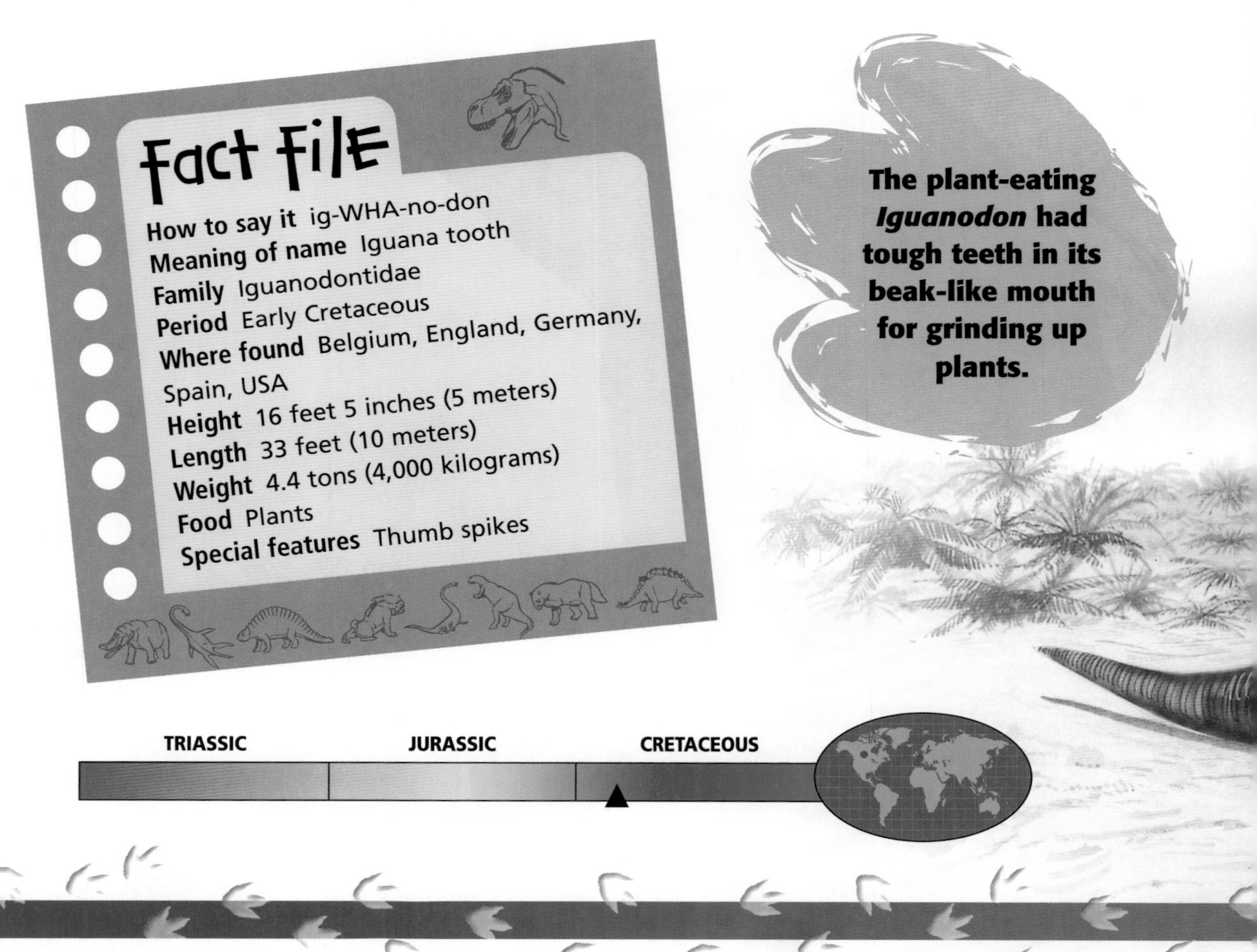

A good sense of taste and smell

Iguanodon wasn't particularly clever, but studies of its brain show it had very well-developed olfactory lobes, which are the areas of the brain that deal with smells. This means that *Iguanodon* had a good sense of smell, handy for sniffing out the tastiest plants—or a nearby predator!

SEISMOSAURUS

***Seismosaurus* was a real record breaker—many paleontologists believe it was the longest of all the dinosaurs at around one third of the length of an American football field. The first remains were discovered in New Mexico, in 1979.**

Short legs

Seismosaurus might have been the longest dinosaur, but it wasn't the tallest by any means, because of its relatively short legs. These stumpy legs (and the front ones were shorter than those at the back) might have helped to make *Seismosaurus* a little more stable—a good thing, since you wouldn't have wanted one of these creatures falling on you.

Longest of all

At around 110 feet (40 meters), *Seismosaurus* was a very long dinosaur indeed, and the longest animal ever to have lived. When a herd of these giants were on the move, you could guarantee that the front of the group would be far ahead of the back.

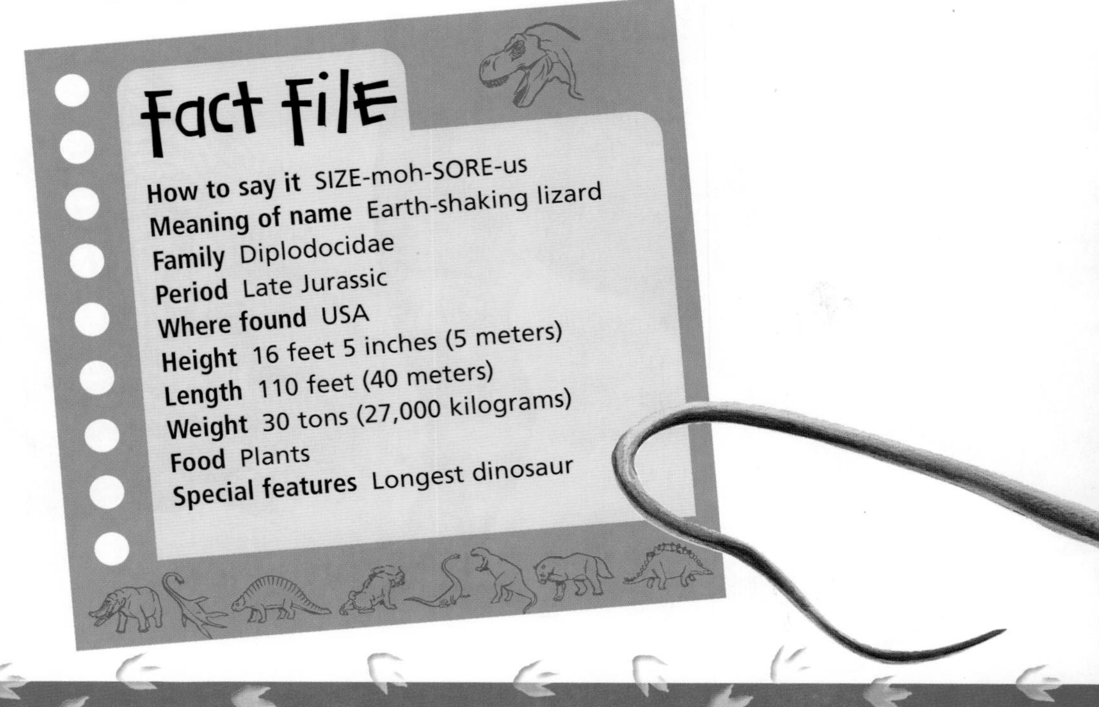

Fact File

How to say it SIZE-moh-SORE-us
Meaning of name Earth-shaking lizard
Family Diplodocidae
Period Late Jurassic
Where found USA
Height 16 feet 5 inches (5 meters)
Length 110 feet (40 meters)
Weight 30 tons (27,000 kilograms)
Food Plants
Special features Longest dinosaur

Too big for forests

Like its cousin, *Diplodocus*, *Seismosaurus* had a long neck. In addition to allowing it to graze over a large area without moving, this also allowed the dinosaur to nose around in places its bulky body prevented it from going, such as in between trees.

Peg-like teeth

Seismosaurus had peg-like teeth, like *Diplodocus*. These were ideal for stripping vegetation from trees or low-lying shrubs, but they were not so good for chewing up food. As a result, *Seismosaurus* swallowed the leaves and stems more or less whole.

SALTASAURUS

The range of dinosaurs that lived in Argentina is very different from that on other continents. *Saltasaurus,* a relatively small sauropod discovered in northwest Argentina, is a good example.

Fact File

How to say it salt-a-SORE-us
Meaning of name Salta lizard
Family Titanosauridae
Period Late Cretaceous
Where found Argentina, Uruguay
Height 16 feet 5 inches (5 meters)
Length 40 feet (12 meters)
Weight 7.7 tons (7,000 kilograms)
Food Plants
Special features Armor plating

Something extra

Saltasaurus was much like any other sauropod: a long neck and tail, small head, big body, and so on. But it had something else as well—armor plating. Its back was covered with small, bony plates and bumps which were a useful defense against attack. Since *Saltasaurus* was one of the smaller sauropods, any extra protection had to be welcome.

Protective mothers

When it was time to lay their eggs, *Saltasaurus* mothers dug holes in the earth to create nesting sites. They laid their eggs in the holes and then covered them over with soil for incubation. When the young hatched, the adults would protect them from any predators who approached in the hope of finding an easy meal.

APATOSAURUS

***Apatosaurus* was a huge sauropod, one of the biggest types of dinosaur. Its sheer size was enough to put off most predators, and its long neck was excellent for grazing plants and leaves beyond the reach of other herbivores.**

Mistaken identity

Until fairly recently, the most complete *Apatosaurus* skeleton ever found was thought to belong to an entirely different species of dinosaur. In 1879, shortly after its discovery, it was named *Brontosaurus*. However, experts have finally proved that the skeleton in fact belongs to *Apatosaurus*, and so the name "Brontosaurus" has been dropped.

Water-dweller?

The nostrils of *Apatosaurus* were located on the top of its head. In the past, some people believed it might have lived in water, like a hippopotamus. This seemed to make sense—the water would have helped support the dinosaur's massive body and *Apatosaurus* could have breathed by sticking the top of its head out of the water. However, we now have firm evidence that this dinosaur was a land-dweller.

Fact File

How to say it a-PAT-oh-SORE-us
Meaning of name Deceptive lizard
Family Diplodocidae
Period Late Jurassic
Where found USA
Height 13 feet (4 meters)
Length 69 feet (21 meters)
Weight 33 tons (30,000 kilograms)
Food Plants
Special features Enormous size

A nearly complete *Apatosaurus* skeleton went on show in 1905 at a museum in the USA. It was the first sauropod to be exhibited.

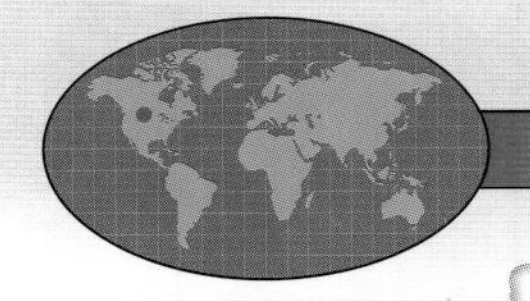

TRIASSIC | JURASSIC | CRETACEOUS

QUAESITOSAURUS

This long-necked sauropod moved in herds across Mongolia. Like its cousin, *Diplodocus*, it had a whiplike tail that it used as a weapon against predators.

Massive muncher

Quaesitosaurus, like all the large sauropods, had to consume a huge amount of food every day just to keep going. For a big dinosaur, it only had a little mouth, so those jaws worked hard every day, especially since leaves are not always the most nutritious of foods. These dinosaurs spent most of their time eating.

Stomach stones

Many plant-eating dinosaurs—*Quaesitosaurus* included—carried gastroliths in their stomachs. These are stones that the dinosaur swallowed to help grind up the food inside its stomach. Today, some birds, such as chickens, do this too.

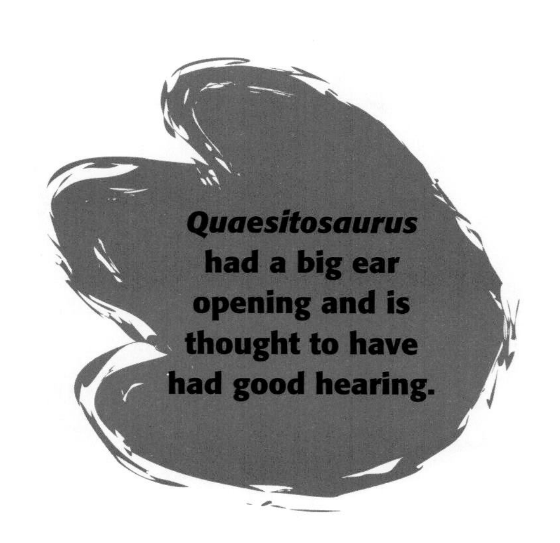

TRIASSIC | JURASSIC | CRETACEOUS

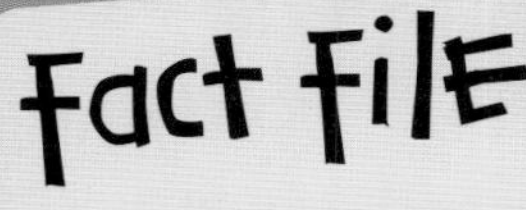

Fact File

How to say it kway-zee-tuh-SORE-us
Meaning of name Abnormal lizard
Family Diplodocidae
Period Late Cretaceous
Where found Mongolia
Height 25 feet (7.6 meters)
Length 66 feet (20 meters)
Weight Not known
Food Plants
Special features Whiplike tail

Picture credits

© Shutterstock front and back cover.

© De Agostini Picture Library: title page; page 4; page 5; pages 8–9; pages 10–11; pages 12–13; pages 14–15; pages 16–17; pages 18–19; pages 20–21; pages 22–23; pages 28–29

© Miles Kelly Publishing Ltd: pages 26–27

© Highlights for Children, Inc: pages 6–7; pages 24–25

This edition published in 2013 by Arcturus Publishing Limited
26/27 Bickels Yard, 151–153 Bermondsey Street,
London SE1 3HA

ISBN: 978-1-84858-765-6
CH002610US
Supplier 15, Date 1012, Print run 2167

Printed in China